SMART DIY: BOOK IV

The Permit Shortcut:

How Smart Homeowners Get ADU Approvals Fast in LA, Orange County & San Diego

Smart DIY - Volume IV

Written by Thomas Quirk
Edited by Angélica Díaz
Review and Design by Angélica Díaz

First Edition: 2026
Production:

SMART DIY: BOOK IV

The Permit Shortcut:

How Smart Homeowners Get ADU Approvals Fast in LA, Orange County & San Diego

CONTENT

INTRODUCTION

The Great Disconnect: State Law vs. City Hall

The decision to build an Accessory Dwelling Unit (ADU) in Southern California usually begins with optimism. That optimism is fueled by state laws that promise a simpler process, less red tape, and faster approvals, making ADUs appear straightforward on paper.

The reality, however, is very different. Most homeowners collide with local bureaucracy—unclear requirements, inconsistent interpretations, and delays that seem to contradict the very laws meant to protect them.

This gap between state intent and city-level execution is what we call the *Great Disconnect*. In real ADU projects, the permitting phase often becomes the most expensive, time-consuming, and emotionally draining part of the entire build.

Homeowners frequently find themselves trapped in a slow grind of vague plan check comments with no clear path to resolution. Late-discovered utility requirements and repeated submissions and rejections stall momentum. Weeks turn into months, budgets stretch, and confidence erodes—often leaving homeowners feeling powerless, even when the law is on their side.

Permit delays don't just waste time. They increase design fees, extend carrying costs, and force rushed decisions later. This is why this guide exists: to remove that powerlessness.

This is not a checklist or a simple summary of code requirements. It is a strategic manual designed to expose the unwritten rules of permitting, decode how cities actually operate, and help homeowners move projects forward deliberately.

Nearly every delayed ADU permit can be traced back to three root causes: incomplete submissions that fail to answer what reviewers actually care about, cryptic plan check comments that trigger endless revisions, or utility conflicts involving sewer, water, power, or fire requirements. Utility issues alone are the single most common cause of multi-month delays.

California law requires cities to approve or deny a compliant ADU application within 60 days. That timeline is achievable—but only when homeowners understand how to submit complete applications, respond strategically to plan check comments, identify and neutralize utility issues early, and enforce their rights when necessary.

Permitting is not administrative. It is strategic. Homeowners who approach it intentionally, rather than passively, experience fewer resubmittals, fewer surprises, and dramatically shorter approval timelines.

Ultimately, this guide is about understanding the system well enough to protect your time and money, keep your ADU project alive and moving, and replace frustration with leverage. Because when you understand the game, you stop feeling stuck—and when you stop feeling stuck, you can win it.

PART I

ASSEMBLING YOUR PERMIT-READY PACKAGE

CHAPTER 1

YOUR RIGHTS AS A HOMEOWNER: LEVERAGING STATE LAW

Your most powerful tool in the ADU permitting process is **not** your architect.

It's **not** your contractor.

It is a clear understanding of **California state law**.

Over the past several years, the state has passed aggressive ADU legislation designed to **force local jurisdictions to approve ADUs with minimal friction**. These laws were written specifically because cities were blocking housing through delay, subjectivity, and overreach.

These laws are **not suggestions**.

They are **your rights**.

> *Homeowners who understand state ADU law experience fewer delays, fewer redesigns, and far less pushback from planning departments.*

This chapter breaks down the legal provisions that shift power **back to you**—and shows you how to use them.

Ministerial Approval: Your Shield Against Subjectivity

California law requires that ADU applications be processed through **ministerial approval**.

This one term changes everything.

What "Ministerial Approval" Means in Plain English

If your ADU plans meet **objective**, black-and-white standards in:

- State ADU law
- The building code
- Zoning ordinances (where not preempted by the state)

The city must approve your application.

They may **not** deny or delay your project based on:

- "Neighborhood character"
- Aesthetics or architectural style
- Neighbor objections
- Personal preferences of a plan checker
- Discretionary judgment calls

There are:

- No public hearings
- No discretionary review boards
- No subjective opinions

Your project is judged ***only*** on technical compliance.

Ministerial approval removes emotion and politics from the process. If your plans comply, approval is not optional.

The 60-Day Shot Clock: How the State Forces Action

To prevent endless delays, California law created a **mandatory review timeline**.

Under **California Government Code §65852.2**, a city must **approve or deny** a complete ADU application within **60 days**.

> If they fail to act, the application is ***deemed approved by law.***

When the Clock Starts (This Is Critical)

The 60-day clock begins **only after** the city deems your application **complete**.

That's why:

- Incomplete submissions are so dangerous
- Vague "missing items" comments are often used to delay

If the city returns your application as incomplete:

- The clock does **not** start
- The city gains more time

The Real Bottleneck

Cities don't usually delay approvals—they delay *completeness*. That's where strategy matters.

How to Enforce the 60-Day Rule

If 60 days pass after your application is deemed complete and:

- No approval is issued
- No formal denial is issued

You (or your representative) should send a **formal letter** citing the statute and stating that the application is now **deemed approved**.

In practice, this often triggers:

- Immediate review
- Sudden approval
- Escalation to supervisors

Cities rarely ignore a homeowner who cites the correct statute and timeline in writing.

The State's Non-Negotiable Standards: Your Design Guardrails

California law establishes **minimum ADU standards** that local jurisdictions **cannot make more restrictive**. These standards exist to ensure ADUs are feasible on almost any lot.

When your design complies with these state minimums, your project becomes **legally difficult to deny**—even if local staff dislike it.

This is why designing *to state law*, not just local preference, is a strategic advantage.

> The closer your design aligns with state minimums, the less leverage a city has to push back

What You Should Understand Now

- ☐ State ADU law overrides conflicting local rules
- ☐ Ministerial approval removes subjective judgment
- ☐ Cities cannot deny compliant ADUs based on opinion
- ☐ The 60-day review period is enforceable
- ☐ A "complete" application starts the clock
- ☐ Written communication matters

Immediate Actions

1. **Learn the phrase "ministerial approval"**
   You will use it often.
2. **Ask when your application is deemed complete**
   Get the date in writing.
3. **Track the 60-day deadline yourself**
   Do not rely on the city to do it.
4. **Document everything**
   Emails, dates, names, and comments.

Scripts You Can Use With Planning Departments

When Facing Subjective Pushback

"Can you point me to the objective code section that requires this change under ministerial review?"

When the Process Drags On

"Can you confirm the date my application was deemed complete for purposes of the 60-day review period under Government Code §65852.2?"

Red-Flag Statement

"That's just our local policy."

State law outranks local policy.

Sample Letter: Asserting Your State Law Rights

(Plain-English, firm, and professional)

[Your Name]
[Your Address]
[Date]

[Planning Director's Name]
[City/County Planning Department]
[Address]

Subject: Assertion of State ADU Law Rights — [Your Property Address]

Dear [Director's Name],

This letter concerns our Accessory Dwelling Unit (ADU) application submitted on **[date]** for the property located at **[address]**.

We have received comments from your department requesting **[describe the request, e.g., "a 10-foot rear setback"]**, which we believe conflicts with California state law governing ADUs.

Under **California Government Code §65852.2**, local agencies may not impose standards more restrictive than those established by the state. State law explicitly permits a **minimum 4-foot side and rear setback** for ADUs. Our proposed design complies with this requirement and therefore preempts conflicting local standards.

Additionally, our application was deemed complete on **[date]**. As of today, **[number] days** have elapsed. We respectfully remind the department of the **60-day review period** mandated by state law and request approval based on compliance with objective standards.

We appreciate your prompt attention and look forward to resolution of this matter.

Sincerely,
[Your Name]

Permitting is not about being confrontational.
It's about being **informed, precise, and persistent**.

When you understand state ADU law, the process stops feeling arbitrary. You gain leverage, clarity, and confidence—and the city understands that you are not guessing.

Knowledge doesn't just protect your project.
It moves it forward.

CHAPTER 2

THE PRE-APPLICATION CHECKLIST: BUILDING AN UNDENIABLE SUBMISSION

The most common reason ADU permits get delayed is not zoning complexity or strict inspectors.

It's a simple, avoidable mistake: **an incomplete application**.

When a city receives an incomplete submission, they do **not** conduct a full review. Instead, they perform a quick intake check, issue a rejection notice, and send the application back. When that happens, the official review timeline never starts. You can lose weeks—or even months—without making any real progress.

This chapter exists to make sure that never happens to you.

> Most permit delays happen before the city ever looks at your design.

The goal is simple: submit an application that is so complete, organized, and professional that the city has no reason to reject it—and must begin the formal review process immediately.

The Core Documents: The Backbone of Your Application

These documents are **non-negotiable**. If any one of them is missing, incomplete, or inconsistent, your application will almost certainly be rejected.

> Permit intake is binary: ***complete or rejected.*** There is no "almost."

1. Architectural Plans

Architectural plans explain **what you are building and where**. They are the primary documents the city uses to understand your project.

A complete architectural plan set must include:

Site Plan

A detailed overhead view showing:

- Property lines and dimensions
- Location of the ADU
- Required setbacks
- Existing structures
- Utility connections
- Easements or recorded restrictions

This is often the *first* sheet a reviewer checks.

Floor Plans

Clear interior layouts showing:

- All rooms and spaces
- Doors and windows
- Wall locations
- Dimensions

Ambiguity here almost always triggers comments.

Exterior Elevations

Views of **all four sides** of the ADU showing:

- Exterior materials
- Roof shape and slope
- Window and door styles

These are used to confirm height limits and exterior compliance.

Building Sections

A "cut-through" drawing from ground to roof showing:

- Floor-to-ceiling heights
- Roof structure
- Foundation relationship

Sections answer questions reviewers don't want to ask twice.

2. Structural Engineering Plans

Structural plans prove your ADU is safe—especially critical in earthquake-prone Southern California.

These plans must be **prepared and stamped by a California-licensed structural engineer** and typically include:

Foundation Plan

Showing:

- Foundation type
- Dimensions and depth
- Rebar size and spacing

Framing Plan

Showing:

- Wall framing
- Roof framing
- Structural lumber sizes and spacing

Shear Wall Plan

A critical seismic document identifying:

- Walls resisting lateral forces
- Required nailing patterns
- Hold-downs and metal connectors

> Inspectors will enforce these details exactly—not "close enough."

3. Title 24 Energy Report

The Title 24 report proves compliance with California energy efficiency standards.

Prepared by a **certified energy consultant**, this report becomes part of your approved plans and specifies:

- Required insulation levels
- Window performance (U-factor & SHGC)
- HVAC efficiency requirements

What you install **must match this report**—or inspections will fail.

> Title 24 issues cause more failed inspections than most homeowners expect.

Supporting Reports:
Solve Problems Before the City Finds Them

Not every property requires these reports—but when they are required, missing them causes major delays. Including them proactively signals professionalism.

Soils / Geotechnical Report

Often required if your property:

- Is on a slope
- Is in a landslide or seismic zone
- Has expansive or unstable soil

This report:

- Analyzes soil conditions
- Recommends foundation design

Topographical Survey

A professional survey showing:

- Exact property boundaries
- Elevation changes
- Slopes and drainage

Especially helpful for setback verification and sloped lots.

Tree Report

If construction is near a large or protected tree, the city may require:

- A report from a certified arborist
- Confirmation that construction will not damage the tree

> Tree issues can stop a permit cold if discovered late.

Utility Coordination: Don't Wait to Be Asked

One of the smartest moves you can make is addressing utilities **before** the city raises concerns.

Contact your local:

- Water provider
- Sewer provider
- Electric utility

Request **"Will Serve" letters** confirming:

- Utility capacity for the ADU
- Required upgrades or connection fees

Including these letters shows the city you've already handled one of the **most common delay triggers**.

> Utility conflicts cause the longest permit delays—often measured in months.

The Master Pre-Submission Checklist

Before you submit, confirm:

- ☐ Complete architectural plans
- ☐ Structural plans stamped by CA engineer
- ☐ Title 24 energy report included
- ☐ Soils report (if applicable)
- ☐ Topographic survey (if applicable)
- ☐ Tree report (if applicable)
- ☐ Utility "Will Serve" letters
- ☐ All documents consistent with each other

> If one box is unchecked, **do not submit**.

Do This Now: Immediate Actions

1. Ask your designer for a **submission checklist**
2. Verify all plans reference the same site conditions
3. Confirm all reports are finalized—not "in progress"
4. Organize documents in a clean, logical order
5. Submit as a single, professional package

Scripts & Questions You Can Use

To your designer or architect

"Is this package complete enough to be accepted on first intake?"

To the city planning counter

"Can you confirm this meets the requirements for a complete ADU submittal?"

To yourself

"Am I submitting something I'd approve if I were the reviewer?"

Final Thought

When you submit a complete and organized permit package, you're doing more than filing paperwork.

You are signaling that your project is:

- Well planned
- Code compliant
- Ready for serious review

A professional submission doesn't guarantee instant approval—but it **does** force the city to start the clock without delay.

And that alone can save you months.

CHAPTER 3

JURISDICTION DEEP DIVE: THE UNWRITTEN RULES OF LA, OC, AND SAN DIEGO

California state law creates a uniform framework for ADUs—but approval does **not** happen in a vacuum.

On the ground, every major Southern California jurisdiction brings its own:

- Priorities
- Interpretations
- Pain points
- Unwritten rules

Understanding these local realities is the difference between:

- A clean, fast approval
- And months of avoidable back-and-forth

In practice, the fastest ADU permits are not just legally compliant—they are locally fluent.

This chapter breaks down what you are most likely to encounter in **Los Angeles**, **Orange County**, and **San Diego**, so you can tailor your submission instead of reacting to surprises.

Los Angeles (City & County): Fire, Water, and Bureaucracy

Los Angeles is enormous, complex, and process heavy. The two biggest friction points are **fire safety** and **water infrastructure**, compounded by a deeply layered bureaucracy.

Fire Safety and the VHFHSZ

Large portions of Los Angeles fall within the **Very High Fire Hazard Severity Zone (VHFHSZ)**. If your property is in one of these areas, expect heightened scrutiny from the Fire Department.

Common requirements include:

- **Fire-rated construction**
  Non-combustible siding, fire-rated windows, and approved roofing materials.
- **Defensible space and clearance**
  Strict vegetation and brush-clearing rules around the ADU.
- **Fire access**
  Detailed site plan review to confirm fire truck access—often a major challenge for hillside lots and narrow streets.

LA Fire Is a Gatekeeper
In Los Angeles, fire approval is not a formality. It is often the controlling factor in permit timelines.

Water Pressure and LADWP

If your ADU requires **fire sprinklers**, Los Angeles will require proof of adequate water pressure.

This usually means:

- A **Water Flow Test**
- Coordination with LADWP

If pressure is insufficient, the city may require:

- A water line upgrade
- New meters or service changes

> These upgrades can add **tens of thousands of dollars and months of delay**

Navigating LADBS

The Los Angeles Department of Building and Safety (LADBS) uses:

- A complex online portal
- Multiple plan check disciplines
- Limited cross-department coordination

> For many homeowners, a **permit expediter familiar with LADBS** dramatically reduces friction.

In Los Angeles, projects slow down not because they are wrong—but because they are unfamiliar with the system.

Orange County: Coastal Rules, HOAs, and Suburban Resistance

Orange County's challenges are less about fire and more about **overlapping authority** and **local resistance**.

The Coastal Zone Overlay

If your property falls within the **Coastal Zone**, your ADU may require review by the **California Coastal Commission**.

This can:

- Add an extra approval layer
- Reintroduce subjective design considerations
- Extend timelines significantly

In coastal areas, ministerial approval still applies—but it becomes more fragile.

> **Coastal Review Changes the Game**
> Coastal oversight often shifts ADUs from "fast and objective" to "slow and negotiated."

HOA Power (Yes, It Still Matters)

Orange County has a high concentration of **Homeowners Associations (HOAs)**.

While state law limits an HOA's ability to ban ADUs outright, it **does allow enforcement of design standards**, such as:

- Roof materials
- Paint colors
- Window styles
- Architectural consistency

> In many cities, you must obtain **HOA approval before city submission**.
> ***Failing to do so can stall your permit*** before it even enters review.

Suburban Scrutiny

Some affluent OC cities comply with state law reluctantly.

They may:

- Scrutinize details aggressively
- Issue lengthy plan check comments
- Delay through technical interpretation rather than denial

This makes **over-documentation and clarity** essential. In Orange County, compliance alone is not enough—presentation and completeness matter.

San Diego: Infrastructure and Geology Drive Delays

San Diego's permitting challenges stem from **aging infrastructure** and **complex geology**.

Sewer and Water Capacity

San Diego is highly focused on system capacity.

Common requirements include:

- **Capacity fees** for sewer and water
- **Video inspection of existing sewer laterals** (especially for older homes)

If the lateral is damaged:

- You may be required to replace it
- At your expense
- Before permit approval

The Hidden Cost

Sewer issues are one of San Diego's most common—and most expensive—late-stage surprises.

Geological Hazard Zones

With canyons, slopes, and coastal bluffs, many properties fall within **geological hazard zones**.

This often means:

- A standard soils report is not enough
- Additional geotechnical analysis may be required

These reports may address:

- Slope stability
- Seismic risk
- Liquefaction potential

They increase:

- Engineering complexity
- Foundation cost
- Review time

In San Diego, the ground beneath your ADU often matters more than the structure above it.

Why This Local Knowledge Matters

By understanding these jurisdiction-specific pressure points, you can:

- Address them **before submission**
- Reduce plan check cycles
- Signal competence to reviewers
- Shorten approval timelines

Plan checkers move faster when they see:

"This applicant has done their homework."

What You Should Understand Now

- ☐ State law is consistent, but enforcement is not
- ☐ Los Angeles prioritizes fire and water infrastructure
- ☐ Orange County adds complexity through HOAs and coastal rules
- ☐ San Diego focuses on sewer capacity and geology
- ☐ Local strategy speeds up approvals

Immediate Actions

1. **Identify your jurisdiction early**
   City vs. county matters.
2. **Ask what historically slows permits there**
   Not what the checklist says.
3. **Flag fire, water, sewer, and geology issues upfront**
   Don't wait for plan check comments.
4. **Tailor your submission to local priorities**
   Same law—different battlefield.

Scripts You Can Use With Your Design Team

Early Strategy Question

"What issues typically delay ADU permits in this city, and how are we addressing them in the first submission?"

When Submitting

"We've proactively addressed fire, utilities, and site constraints specific to this jurisdiction."

Red-Flag Statement

"We'll deal with that after plan check."

That usually means **delay is already baked in**.

State law gives you the right to build an ADU.

Local knowledge determines **how long it takes**.

When you design and submit with local realities in mind, you stop fighting the process—and start moving through it efficiently.

PART II

SURVIVING THE PLAN CHECK

CHAPTER 4

DECODING THE PLAN CHECK COMMENT LETTER

Receiving your first plan check comment letter from the city is a moment of truth.

For an unprepared homeowner, it can feel like a rejection—a dense list of obstacles written in unfamiliar language. For a strategic homeowner, it is something very different.

It is a **to-do list**.

> *In successful ADU projects, the first plan check letter is not a setback—it's the beginning of the final stretch.*

A comment letter is **not a denial**.
It is a roadmap to approval.

Your ability to **decode it, organize it, and respond to it professionally** will determine how fast your project moves forward.

What a Plan Check Comment Letter Really Is

Plan check comments exist for one purpose:
to identify gaps between your submitted plans and what the city requires for approval.

They are not:

- A judgment on whether your ADU should exist
- A commentary on your design taste
- A sign that the project is failing

They are instructions.

The Mindset Shift
Treat every comment as a task, not a critique. Emotion slows projects. Organization speeds them up.

The Anatomy of a Comment Letter

A typical plan check letter is divided by **reviewing department**. Each department looks at your plans through a very narrow lens.

Understanding this prevents overreaction—and helps you respond efficiently.

Common departments include:

- Planning / Zoning
- Building / Structural
- Fire
- Public Works / Utilities
- Energy / Title 24

Each department only comments on what falls under **their authority**.

Why Comments Interact With Each Other

It's critical to understand that **one comment can trigger changes elsewhere**.

Example:

- Fire Department requires fire sprinklers
- This triggers:
    - Plumbing plan revisions (Building)
    - Water supply verification (Utilities)
    - Possibly a Title 24 update

Comments Are Not Isolated
Solving one comment without checking downstream impacts often leads to new comments in the next round.

The Comment Log: Your Control Center

Do **not** manage plan check responses through scattered emails, memory, or phone calls.

You need a **Comment Log**.

This is a simple spreadsheet that becomes:

- Your master checklist
- Your progress tracker
- Your communication tool

Projects that stall during plan check almost always lack a centralized response system.

What Goes in a Comment Log

Each row should include:

- Department
- Comment number
- Comment text (summarized)
- Required action
- Responsible party (architect, engineer, consultant)
- Status (open / revised / completed)
- Notes

This log becomes the **single source of truth** for your resubmission.

Plan checkers respond faster when they can clearly see that every comment has been tracked and resolved.

The Response Letter: Where Most Homeowners Go Wrong

Your resubmission must include a **formal Response Letter**, usually prepared by your architect or lead designer.

This letter is just as important as the revised drawings.

What the Response Letter Is Not

It is not:

- Defensive
- Argumentative
- Emotional
- A place to debate policy

Even when a comment feels unreasonable, tone matters.

What the Response Letter Should Be

A good response letter is:

- Clear
- Structured
- Direct
- Easy to review

Proper Response Letter Structure

- Organized by **department**
- Mirrors the city's **comment numbers**
- Responds to **every comment**, even if no change was required
- References:
    - Sheet number
    - Detail number
    - Revision cloud

Example format:

Fire Department – Comment 3
Comment: Provide fire sprinkler coverage per code.
Response: Fire sprinklers have been added per CBC requirements. See Sheet FP-1, Details 2 and 4.

This saves the plan checker time—and *time* is what gets approvals.

Make the Reviewer's Job Easy
The easier your response is to verify, the faster it gets approved.

Why Professionalism Speeds Approval

Cities process hundreds of applications.

When your resubmission shows:

- A clean Comment Log
- A structured Response Letter
- Coordinated plan revisions

You signal something important:

"This applicant knows what they're doing."

That perception alone can shorten review cycles.

Well-organized resubmissions often move through review in half the time of disorganized ones—even when the scope is identical.

Chapter Checklist: What You Should Understand Now

- ☐ A comment letter is not a denial
- ☐ Comments are instructions, not opinions
- ☐ Departments review plans independently
- ☐ One comment can trigger others
- ☐ A Comment Log is essential
- ☐ A structured Response Letter speeds approval

Immediate Actions

1. **Create a Comment Log template now**
   Don't wait for your first letter.
2. **Commit to written tracking only**
   No verbal-only resolutions.
3. **Review comments holistically**
   Look for downstream impacts.
4. **Demand a formal Response Letter**
   Every resubmission, every time.

Scripts You Can Use With Your Design Team

Script: After Receiving Comments

"Let's log every comment, identify cross-department impacts, and prepare a clean response letter."

Script: When Reviewing the Resubmission

"Can you show me where each comment is addressed on the plans and referenced in the response letter?"

Red-Flag Statement

"We'll just explain it to them if they ask."

That almost always leads to **another review cycle**.

Plan check comments are not obstacles.
They are **instructions for finishing the race**.

When you treat the comment letter as a project management task—tracked, documented, and professionally resolved—you turn what feels like resistance into forward motion.

> Approval is not about arguing harder.
> It's about responding smarter.

CHAPTER 5

HIGH-PAIN-POINT ISSUE #1: FIRE SPRINKLERS AND WATER PRESSURE

Of all the potential hurdles in the ADU permitting process, **none causes more shock—or more unplanned expense—than fire sprinklers**.

This single requirement can add **tens of thousands of dollars** to a project and months to your timeline. The worst part? Many homeowners don't even realize sprinklers are required until they are deep into permitting, when options are limited and leverage is gone.

In real ADU projects, fire sprinklers are one of the most common causes of sudden, catastrophic budget increases.

This chapter explains **when sprinklers are required**, **why water pressure becomes the real problem**, and **how to investigate the issue early—before it controls your project**.

When Are Fire Sprinklers Required?

Fire sprinkler requirements are not random. They are triggered by specific conditions in the California Fire Code and local fire department policies.

While details vary by jurisdiction, the most common triggers are consistent across Southern California.

Trigger #1: The Main House Is Already Sprinklered

If your primary residence already has a fire sprinkler system, **any new ADU must also be sprinklered**.

This applies to:

- Attached ADUs
- Detached ADUs

> There is no workaround. The ADU must match the life-safety system of the main house.

Trigger #2: Distance From a Fire Hydrant (Detached ADUs)

For detached ADUs, the most common trigger is **distance to the nearest public fire hydrant**.

If the ADU is farther than the allowed distance—often **around 150 feet** (but determined locally)—the fire department may require sprinklers to compensate for slower response time.

Trigger #3: Fire Department Access

If a fire truck cannot get close enough to the ADU because of:

- A long driveway
- Narrow access roads
- Hillside conditions

> Sprinklers may be required as a **life-safety substitute** for limited access.

Why Sprinklers Feel Arbitrary
The rule isn't "all ADUs need sprinklers." The rule is "when access or response time is limited, sprinklers replace what fire trucks can't do."

The Water Flow Test: Where Cost Becomes Real

Once sprinklers are required, the real issue is **not the sprinklers themselves**.

It's **water pressure**.

Before approving the permit, the Fire Department will require a **Water Flow Test** to prove your property can supply enough water to operate the sprinkler system.

What the Water Flow Test Involves

The test must be performed by:

- A licensed fire protection engineer, or
- A C-16 fire protection contractor

The process includes:

- Opening a nearby fire hydrant
- Measuring water flow (gallons per minute)
- Measuring residual pressure (pressure left while water is flowing)

These readings are then analyzed to determine whether your water supply can meet sprinkler demand under fire conditions.

Most sprinkler problems are not design problems—they are infrastructure problems.

The Nightmare Scenario: Insufficient Water Pressure

If the Water Flow Test shows your pressure is insufficient, the Fire Department **will not approve your permit** until the issue is resolved.

At that point, your options are limited—and expensive.

Option 1: Water Line Upgrade

This involves replacing the existing water service line from the street to your property with a larger pipe.

What this means in reality:

- Trenching in the public right-of-way
- Coordination with the local water utility
- Traffic control and restoration
- Long approval timelines

Typical cost: $20,000–$50,000
Typical delay: Several months

Option 2: Booster Pump and Storage Tank

An alternative solution is installing:

- A dedicated water storage tank
- A booster pump that increases pressure during a fire

This avoids upgrading the street connection but introduces:

- Equipment cost
- Ongoing maintenance
- Space loss on your property

Typical cost: $10,000–$20,000

Why This Is So Painful
These costs often appear *after* design is complete—when changing direction is expensive and emotionally exhausting.

The Strategic Approach: Investigate Early or Pay Later

Because of the massive financial impact, **fire sprinkler feasibility must be evaluated early**, not after permit submission.

Step 1: Confirm Whether Sprinklers Are Required

Have your architect or designer:

- Confirm sprinkler requirements directly with the Fire Department
- Document the determination in writing

Never assume.

Step 2: Perform a Preliminary Water Analysis

If sprinklers are likely, hire a fire protection professional **before finalizing plans** to:

- Review available water supply
- Identify potential pressure issues early

This step alone can save **tens of thousands of dollars**.

> Homeowners who investigate sprinkler feasibility early rarely experience catastrophic permit surprises.

What You Should Understand Now

- ☐ Fire sprinklers are triggered by specific conditions
- ☐ Detached ADUs are commonly affected by hydrant distance
- ☐ Water pressure—not sprinklers—is the real cost driver
- ☐ Insufficient pressure can require major infrastructure upgrades
- ☐ Early investigation protects both budget and timeline

Immediate Actions

1. **Ask explicitly whether sprinklers are required**
   Get a clear answer early.
2. **Identify the nearest fire hydrant**
   Distance matters.
3. **Flag access limitations**
   Long driveways and narrow roads are red flags.
4. **Budget conservatively if sprinklers are likely**
   Hope is not a strategy.

Scripts You Can Use Immediately

Script: With Your Architect

"Before we finalize the design, can you confirm with the Fire Department whether sprinklers are required for this ADU?"

Script: With a Fire Protection Professional

"Can you perform a preliminary water flow analysis to identify any pressure issues before we submit plans?"

Red-Flag Statement

"We'll deal with sprinklers after plan check."

That usually means **the most expensive option will be the only option**.

Fire sprinklers are not a design preference—they are a **life-safety requirement tied to infrastructure reality**.

When you investigate early, they become a manageable budget line.
When you ignore them, they become a financial ambush.

This chapter isn't meant to scare you.
It's meant to ensure **you are never surprised by the most expensive line item you didn't plan for**.

CHAPTER 6

HIGH-PAIN-POINT ISSUE #2: UTILITY UPGRADES AND FEES

While the building department is reviewing your architectural and structural plans, a **second, equally critical process** is unfolding quietly in the background.

It involves your:

- Sewer provider
- Water district
- Power company
- Gas utility

Their approvals are **not building code issues.**
They are **infrastructure issues.**

And they are one of the most common reasons an ADU project stalls—even after the building permit is technically ready.

> *In real ADU projects, utility signoffs are the number one cause of "everything is approved, but nothing can start."*

This chapter breaks down the second major high-pain-point of permitting: **utility upgrades, capacity fees, and long lead times**—and how to manage them before they control your schedule.

Sewer: Capacity Fees and the Lateral Replacement Trap

Before your ADU can be approved, the city's public works or sanitation department must confirm that the public sewer system can handle the additional wastewater from your new unit.

This review often uncovers **two expensive surprises**.

1. Sewer Capacity Fees *(A Mandatory Soft Cost)*

Most jurisdictions charge a **one-time Sewer Capacity Fee** to connect a new ADU to the public system.

This fee:

- Is non-negotiable
- Is paid before final approval
- Exists to fund future sewer expansion and maintenance

> **Typical range:** A few thousand dollars: Up to **$10,000+**, depending on jurisdiction

Why This Fee Feels So Shocking
Capacity fees don't improve your property—they fund the system. That's why homeowners rarely expect them.

You must request a **written fee estimate** from your local sanitation district early, or this cost will surface late—when it's hardest to absorb.

2. Sewer Lateral Condition *(The Older-Home Surprise)*

For older homes (typically built **before 1980**), many cities require proof that your existing **sewer lateral**—the pipe connecting your house to the main sewer line—is in good condition.

This requires a **video inspection**, where a camera is run through the pipe.

If the inspection reveals:

- Cracks
- Root intrusion
- Collapsed or broken clay pipe

you will be required to **replace the entire lateral**—at your expense.

Typical cost: $5,000–$15,000

Sewer lateral replacements are one of the most common and least budgeted-for utility costs in ADU projects.

Power: The 200-Amp Upgrade and Utility Timelines

An ADU adds a major electrical load—kitchen appliances, HVAC, lighting, and possibly EV charging.

The key question is simple:
Can your existing electrical service handle it?

The Main Service Upgrade

Many older homes have:

- 100-amp service
- 125-amp service

This is often **insufficient** to safely power both the main house and an ADU.

As a result, many projects require:

- A **200-amp main service panel upgrade**

This work:

- Must be performed by a licensed electrician
- Typically costs **$3,000–$7,000**

The Upgrade Is Only Half the Problem
The electrician can do the work—but the ***utility controls the timeline.***

Utility Company Lead Times

A service upgrade requires coordination with your power provider (such as Southern California Edison or SDG&E).

They must:

- De-energize your home
- Inspect the new panel
- Re-energize the system

The problem is timing.

Typical utility lead time:
4 to 8 weeks (sometimes longer)

If you wait until the ADU is finished to start this process, you may end up with:

- A fully built unit
- No power
- Weeks of delay

Many ADUs sit complete—but unusable—because the utility upgrade was started too late.

Gas: The Meter and Capacity Question

If your ADU will use natural gas—for:

- A furnace
- A water heater
- A gas stove

you will need to extend gas service from the main house.

In some cases, the gas utility may require:

- A **separate gas meter** for the ADU

This adds:

- Cost
- Permitting complexity
- Coordination with the gas company

This requirement varies by utility and must be confirmed early.

Don't Assume "Same Meter"
Meter requirements are utility decisions—not design preferences.

The Strategic Approach: Run Utilities in Parallel

The biggest mistake homeowners make is treating utilities as something that happens *after* building approval.

They are not.

Utilities must be treated as a **parallel permitting track**.

That means:

- Engaging utility providers early
- Requesting written requirements
- Starting upgrades as soon as permits allow

> **The Cost of Waiting**
> A building permit without utility sign-offs is a project that looks approved—but can't move forward.

What You Should Understand Now

- ☐ Utility approvals are separate from building permits
- ☐ Sewer capacity fees are mandatory and often high
- ☐ Older homes may require sewer lateral replacement
- ☐ Electrical service upgrades are common
- ☐ Utility scheduling delays can stall completed projects
- ☐ Gas meter requirements vary by provider

Immediate Actions

1. **Contact your sewer district early**
   Request capacity fee estimates in writing.
2. **Ask whether a sewer video inspection is required**
   Especially if your home is older.
3. **Confirm your electrical service size**
   Don't guess—verify.
4. **Call the power utility about upgrade timelines**
   Build their schedule into yours.
5. **Clarify gas meter requirements early**
   Avoid redesigns later.

Scripts You Can Use Immediately

Script: With the Sewer Department

"Can you provide the sewer capacity fee for an ADU at this address and confirm whether a lateral inspection is required?"

Script: With the Electrician

"Based on this ADU, will a 200-amp service upgrade be required?"

Script: With the Power Company

"What is the current lead time for coordinating a service upgrade once permits are issued?"

Red-Flag Statement

"Utilities usually figure themselves out later."

That usually means **months of delay are already scheduled**.

> Utilities don't care that your ADU is well designed. They care about **capacity, safety, and infrastructure limits**.

When you treat utilities as a separate, parallel process—and start early—you avoid the most frustrating scenario of all: *An approved ADU that can't be used.*

Handled proactively, utility sign-offs stop being a crisis and become just another managed step toward completion.

PART III

FROM APPROVAL TO OCCUPANCY

CHAPTER 7

PERMIT EXPEDITION: YOUR TOOLKIT FOR SPEED

The 60-day rule is a powerful legal backstop—but it should not be your **only** strategy.

You do not have to sit quietly while your application crawls through review. There are practical, professional ways to **move the process forward** by improving communication, removing friction, and escalating only when necessary.

> *In successful ADU projects, approval speed is driven less by pressure—and more by clarity and professionalism.*

The goal is simple:
Make it **easy** for the plan checker to say *Approved*.

The Permit Expediter: The Shortcut Most Homeowners Don't Know Exists

A **Permit Expediter** is a professional who specializes in navigating building department bureaucracy.

They do not design buildings.
They manage systems.

What a Permit Expediter Actually Does

A good expediter will:

- Submit plans correctly the first time
- Pay and track fees
- Monitor your application inside the city's system
- Communicate directly with plan checkers
- Catch formatting or administrative errors that trigger rejections

They understand the **unwritten preferences** of specific departments—knowledge that often saves weeks of delay.

> An expediter doesn't speed up the city—they prevent your project from getting stuck.

When Hiring an Expediter Makes Sense

Consider an expediter if:

- Your architect does not include permit processing
- You are self-managing the project
- You are in a complex jurisdiction (e.g., Los Angeles)
- Your project has already stalled

Typical cost: a few thousand dollars
Typical payoff: faster approvals, fewer resubmittals, less stress

> In large jurisdictions, permit expediters often pay for themselves by preventing avoidable delays.

The Face-to-Face Meeting: The Fastest Way to Break a Deadlock

If your project is stuck in a loop of comments and resubmissions, email is no longer enough.

It's time to **talk to a human**.

Why Meetings Work

A plan check comment that feels impossible on paper is often:

- A misunderstanding
- A missing explanation
- A solvable technical concern

A short meeting can uncover the *real issue*—and resolve it quickly.

Email Creates Distance.
Meetings Create Momentum.

How to Prepare for the Meeting

Bring:

- Your architect or engineer
- Your **Comment Log**
- A clean, marked-up set of plans

Your objective is not to argue.
Your objective is to understand.

How to Approach the Conversation

- Be professional and calm
- Ask clarifying questions
- Focus on solutions, not blame

A **15-minute meeting** can accomplish more than weeks of back-and-forth emails.

Strategic Escalation: When Cooperation Isn't Enough

Most plan checkers want to approve projects—not block them. But occasionally, you will encounter:

- Unresponsiveness
- Misinterpretation of state law
- Endless moving goalposts

When that happens, escalation is appropriate—but only if done **correctly**.

Step 1: Document Everything

Keep records of:

- Emails
- Dates and response times
- Specific comments and corrections

Documentation gives you credibility.

Escalation Without Documentation Is Just Complaining

Step 2: Request a Supervisor Meeting

Your first escalation is **not** a complaint—it's a request for clarity.

Frame it as:

> *"We'd like to ensure we're interpreting the requirements correctly and find a path forward."*

This keeps the tone collaborative.

Step 3: Contact the Building Official

If the issue persists, escalate to the **Building Official**—the head of the department.

This is the final authority.

Use this step sparingly, clearly, and professionally.

Escalation works best when it is calm, factual, and clearly grounded in state law.

The Professional Resubmission: Your Silent Accelerator

Every resubmission is a chance to either:

- Frustrate the reviewer
- Or make their job easy

Choose the second.

What a Strong Resubmission Includes

A professional package should contain:

1. **A concise Response Letter**
   - Addresses every comment
   - Mirrors the city's numbering
   - Points directly to revised sheets
2. **An Updated Comment Log**
   - Shows resolution status clearly
3. **Slip Sheets Only**
   - Include *only* revised drawings
   - No full plan set unless required

> Reviewers Approve What They Can Verify Quickly

What You Should Know Now

- ☐ You don't have to wait passively
- ☐ Permit expediters reduce friction
- ☐ Meetings resolve issues faster than email
- ☐ Escalation must be strategic and documented
- ☐ Professional resubmissions speed approval

Immediate Actions

1. **Assess whether you need an expediter**
   Especially in large jurisdictions.
2. **Prepare for a meeting before frustration builds**
   Early is better than late.
3. **Organize your documentation**
   Assume escalation may be needed.
4. **Upgrade your resubmission quality**
   Every cycle matters.

Scripts You Can Use Immediately

Script: Requesting a Meeting

"We'd like to meet briefly to make sure we fully understand the intent of the comments and address them correctly."

Script: Escalating to a Supervisor

"We're seeking guidance to resolve an interpretation issue and keep the project moving forward."

Script: Framing a Resubmission

"We've addressed each comment directly and highlighted all revisions for ease of review."

Red-Flag Statement

"Just keep resubmitting—it'll eventually get approved."

That usually means **months of avoidable delay**.

Permitting speed is rarely about force.

It's about **clarity, professionalism, and leverage used wisely**.

> When you communicate clearly, organize relentlessly, and escalate only when necessary, you turn the permitting process from a bottleneck into a manageable system.

Approval doesn't come from pushing harder.

It comes from **making it easy to say yes**.

CHAPTER 8

THE INSPECTION SEQUENCE: A FIELD GUIDE FOR YOUR CONTRACTOR

Receiving your building permit is a major milestone. The paperwork phase is over. Construction can finally begin.

But the city is not done with your project.

From this point forward, inspectors will visit the site at specific stages to verify that the work is being built **safely and exactly as approved**. How well these inspections are managed will directly affect your timeline, costs, and stress level.

> *In real ADU projects, delays during construction are far more often caused by failed inspections than by slow building.*

This chapter explains **how inspections work, why their order matters, and how to avoid re-inspection delays**.

The Logic Behind the Inspection Sequence

City inspections follow a simple rule:

Inspect what will soon be hidden.

Inspectors must verify work **before it gets covered up** by the next phase of construction.

For example:

- Rebar must be inspected **before** concrete is poured
- Electrical wiring must be inspected **before** drywall is installed

If work is covered before inspection, it will usually need to be **opened up again at your expense**.

> Never move to the next phase until the current inspection has passed.

The Major Inspections: A Practical Checklist

While names and order may vary slightly by jurisdiction, nearly every ADU project includes the following inspections.

1. Foundation Inspection

Occurs after:

- Forms are set
- Rebar is installed

Inspector checks:

- Footing dimensions
- Rebar size, spacing, and placement

Only after passing can concrete be poured.

2. Framing Inspection

Occurs after:

- Structural framing is complete
- Shear panels, hold-downs, and connectors are installed

Inspector checks:

- Structural layout
- Connections and hardware
- Compliance with structural plans

3. Rough-In Inspections

These often include **separate inspections** for:

- Plumbing
- Electrical
- Mechanical (HVAC)

Occurs after:

- Pipes, wires, and ducts are installed
- Walls are still open

Inspector checks:

- Code compliance
- Clearances
- Proper materials and installation

4. Insulation Inspection *(if required)*

Occurs after:

- Insulation is installed
- Before drywall

Inspector checks:

- R-values
- Coverage and installation quality

5. Drywall Inspection *(in some cities)*

Occurs after:

- Drywall is hung
- Before final finishes

6. Final Inspection

Occurs when:

- Construction is complete
- All fixtures are installed
- Site is clean and safe

Inspector verifies:

- Life-safety items
- Code compliance
- Consistency with approved plans

Passing this inspection is typically required before the **Certificate of Occupancy** is issued.

Most inspection failures happen because the sequence was rushed—not because the work was unsafe.

When an Inspection Fails: Handling a Correction Notice ("Red Tag")

If an inspector finds a code violation or deviation from the approved plans, they will issue a **Correction Notice**, commonly called a **Red Tag**.

This is not a disaster.
It is a set of instructions.

How to Handle a Red Tag Correctly

1. Stop Work

All work related to the failed inspection must stop immediately. Continuing work can lead to fines or additional penalties.

2. Understand the Correction

Read the notice carefully.

If anything is unclear:

- Ask the inspector **before they leave the site**
- Clarify what must be changed to pass

Guessing leads to repeat failures.

3. Perform the Exact Correction

Have the contractor or responsible subcontractor:

- Correct only what is listed
- Follow the plans and code precisely

4. Schedule Re-Inspection

Once corrected:

- Call for re-inspection
- Be aware that most cities charge a **re-inspection fee**

This fee is a powerful incentive to get it right the first time.

Red Tags Are Not Personal
Inspectors are enforcing code—not criticizing your project.

The On-Site Plans Rule *(The Easiest Way to Fail an Inspection)*

The approved plan set and the building permit card **must be on site at all times**.

Inspectors will:

- Compare field work directly to the plans
- Verify that construction matches approved details

If plans are missing:

- The inspector may fail the inspection
- Leave immediately
- Require a paid re-inspection

This is one of the most common—and avoidable—causes of delay.

No Plans = No Inspection

What You Should Know Now

- ☐ Inspections follow a strict sequence
- ☐ Work must be inspected before it's covered
- ☐ Skipping inspections leads to rework and delays
- ☐ Red Tags are instructions, not failures
- ☐ Approved plans must be on site at all times

Immediate Actions

1. **Confirm the inspection sequence with your contractor**
   Make sure everyone agrees on the order.
2. **Schedule inspections early**
   Inspectors' calendars fill quickly.
3. **Keep plans and permit card on site**
   No exceptions.
4. **Attend key inspections if possible**
   Hearing comments firsthand prevents mistakes.

Scripts You Can Use on the Job Site

Script: With Your Contractor

"Let's confirm we've passed inspection before moving to the next phase."

Script: With an Inspector (If Clarification Is Needed)

"Can you clarify exactly what needs to be corrected so we can address it correctly the first time?"

Red-Flag Statement

"We'll fix it later if they say something."

That almost always leads to **re-inspection fees and lost time**.

Inspections are not obstacles.
They are **checkpoints**.

When you respect the sequence, prepare the site, and respond professionally to corrections, inspections become routine—not stressful.

Handled correctly, they keep your ADU moving steadily toward completion, approval, and occupancy—without unnecessary delays or costly rework.

CHAPTER 9

THE FINAL HURDLE: THE CERTIFICATE OF OCCUPANCY

After weeks of plan check and months of construction, you've reached the final step of the ADU journey: securing the **Certificate of Occupancy (C of O)**.

This single document is the payoff for everything you've done.

It is the city's official declaration that your ADU is:

- **Safe**
- **Code-compliant**
- **Legal for human habitation**

In real ADU projects, the last 5% of work determines whether the unit becomes a legal asset—or an expensive liability.

This chapter walks you through the **final inspection**, the **administrative close-out**, and why the C of O matters more than any other piece of paper you'll receive.

Before You Call the Final Inspection: Do Your Own Punch List

Calling for a final inspection before the unit is truly finished is one of the most common—and costly—mistakes homeowners make.

Before you schedule the inspector, you and your contractor should conduct a **meticulous punch-list walk-through**, using the inspector's perspective.

Final Inspection Punch List (Inspector's View)

Life Safety

- Smoke detectors installed and working
- Carbon monoxide detectors installed and working
- Egress windows and doors open, close, and latch properly
- Handrails and guardrails are secure and correctly sized

Fixtures and Appliances

- All plumbing fixtures installed and leak-free
- Toilets flush properly; hot and cold water function
- Electrical outlets, switches, and light fixtures work
- Built-in appliances installed and operational

Exterior and Site Conditions

- Site clean and free of construction debris
- Exterior outlets and lighting weather-protected
- Final grading directs water away from the foundation
- ADU address numbers clearly visible from the street

> If it's not finished, don't call the inspection. Almost every premature final inspection results in a failure and a paid re-inspection.

The Final Inspection: What the Inspector Is Checking

The final inspection is a **verification**, not a discovery process.

The inspector is confirming that:

- All prior corrections were completed
- The unit matches the approved plans
- Life-safety systems are in place
- The ADU is ready for occupancy

If everything passes, the inspector will **sign off the final inspection** on your permit card.

Final inspections rarely fail because of major issues—they fail because of unfinished details.

Closing Out the Permit: The Administrative Finish Line

Passing the final inspection does **not automatically** produce a Certificate of Occupancy.

You must still **close out the permit** with the building department.

This step is administrative—but essential.

What "Closing Out" Typically Involves

1. **Submit the Signed Permit Card**
   Provide the city with the original permit card showing final inspection approval.
2. **Pay All Outstanding Fees**
   Confirm that all permit fees, impact fees, and re-inspection fees (if any) are paid in full.
3. **Submit Final Paperwork**
   Some cities require final affidavits, energy compliance confirmations, or utility sign-offs.

Only after this process is complete will the city issue the **Certificate of Occupancy**.

Don't Assume It's Automatic
Many projects stall here because the homeowner assumes the city will "take care of it."

Why the Certificate of Occupancy Matters So Much

The C of O is not ceremonial.

It unlocks the **legal and financial value** of your ADU.

Legal Status

Without a C of O:

- The ADU is considered **illegal**
- You cannot legally rent it
- You risk fines, enforcement actions, or occupancy orders

Insurance Coverage

Insurance companies will not properly cover:

- Unpermitted structures
- Units without a C of O

The C of O allows you to:

- Insure the ADU for fire and liability
- Protect yourself financially

Appraisal and Resale Value

When you refinance or sell:

- A permitted ADU with a C of O adds **significant appraised value**
- An unpermitted unit adds little—or can complicate the sale

From a lender's perspective, an ADU without a C of O effectively does not exist.

What You Should Confirm Before Celebrating

- ☐ The ADU passed final inspection
- ☐ All punch-list items are complete
- ☐ The permit is formally closed out
- ☐ All fees are paid
- ☐ The Certificate of Occupancy has been issued

Immediate Actions

1. **Schedule a pre-final walk-through**
   Fix issues before the inspector sees them.
2. **Confirm all paperwork requirements**
   Ask the building department what's needed for close-out.
3. **Track the C of O issuance**
   Don't assume it's automatic.
4. **Store the C of O safely**
   You will need it for insurance, appraisal, and resale.

Scripts You Can Use at the Finish Line

Script: With Your Contractor

"Let's confirm everything on the final inspection checklist is complete before we call it in."

Script: With the Building Department

"What steps are required to close out the permit and issue the Certificate of Occupancy?"

Red-Flag Statement

"We'll deal with the C of O later."

That's how finished projects stay legally unfinished.

The Certificate of Occupancy is the moment your ADU stops being a construction project and becomes a **legal home**.

It is proof that you navigated the system correctly—from permits to inspections to final approval. And it is the key that transforms your investment into a **safe, insurable, income-producing, and fully recognized asset**.

Once you have the C of O in hand, the journey through bureaucracy is over.

What remains is the benefit of having done it right.

CONCLUSION

The Permit is Not the End, It's the Beginning

You have navigated the Great Disconnect between state law and city hall. You assembled an undeniable permit package, survived plan check, managed inspections, and reached the finish line with a Certificate of Occupancy in your hand—a document that is more than approval. It proves you did what most homeowners never do: you finished.

In one of the most challenging regulatory environments in the country, you moved a project from concept to legal reality. And while this may feel like the end of your ADU journey, it is actually the beginning of everything the ADU was meant to deliver.

The permit is the legal foundation beneath every financial and lifestyle benefit your ADU can now provide. It gives you the ability to rent with confidence, house family safely, add real, appraisable value to your property, insure the structure properly, and operate without enforcement risk or future disputes.

What you accomplished goes far beyond construction. You learned how to interpret codes, enforce your rights under state law, manage bureaucracy strategically, and communicate professionally with agencies. You learned how to protect your time, money, and leverage—skills that will serve you in future projects, refinances, negotiations, and property decisions.

With the Certificate of Occupancy issued, the shift is complete. You are no longer asking for permission; you are exercising your rights. Your ADU is now legal, defensible, insurable, and valuable.

The permit maze is behind you. From this point forward, you are no longer navigating bureaucracy—you are managing an asset. One whose income potential, flexibility, security, and long-term value are just beginning, backed by the confidence that comes from knowing the system now works for you.

Made in United States
Troutdale, OR
11/03/2026

56844697R00055